Watery Worlds

DEEP SEA LIFE

Jinny Johnson

A+

Smart Apple Media

Published by Smart Apple Media
P.O. Box 3263
Mankato, MN 56002

Printed in the United States of America at Corporate Graphics,
in North Mankato, Minnesota.

Library of Congress Cataloging-in-Publication Data
Johnson, Jinny, 1949-
 Deep sea life / Jinny Johnson.
    p. cm. -- (Watery worlds)
 Includes index.
 Summary: "Highlights animals that thrive in the deep sea, below where sunlight reaches,
 including deep sea fish, sperm whales, and sea bed creatures that
 have adapted to deep sea life. Includes ocean map and geographical information"
 --Provided by publisher.
 ISBN 978-1-59920-503-8 (library bound)
 1. Deep-sea animals--Juvenile literature. 2. Deep-sea ecology--Juvenile literature.
 I. Title.
 QL125.5.J63 2012
 591.77--dc22

                                                  2011000001

Created by Appleseed Editions, Ltd.
Designed by Hel James
Illustrations by Graham Rosewarne
Edited by Mary-Jane Wilkins
Picture research by Su Alexander

Picture credits
Title page & contents page Phase4Photography/Shutterstock; 4 Oxford Scientific/Photolibrary;
5 Bettmann/Corbis; 6 Marevision//Photolibrary; 7t Oceans-Image/Photoshot/NHPA, b Kevin
Raskoff; 8 David Shale/Nature Picture Library; 9 Doc White/Nature Picture Library; 10 Paulo de
Oliveira/Photolibrary; 11 Oxford Scientific/Photolibrary; 12 Peter Batson/DeepSeaPhotography.
com; 13t Karen Gowlett-Holmes/Photolibrary, b Peter Batson/DeepSeaPhotography.com; 14
Dante Fenolio/Science Photo Library; 15 Mark Conlin/Photolibrary; 16-17 background Argus/
Shutterstock, 16 Jonathan Bird/Photolibrary; 17 Franco Banfi/Photolibrary; 18-19 background
Phase4Photography/Shutterstock, 18 Jonathan Bird/Photolibrary; 19 Bob Cranston/Photolibrary;
20 The Natural History Museum/Alamy; 21 Florian Graner/Nature Picture Library; 22 Clive
Bromhall/Photolibrary; 23 Doc White/Nature Picture Library; 24 Oceans-Image/Photoshot/
NHPA; 25t Bruce Rasner/Rotman/Nature Picture Library, b Kelvin Aitken/Photolibrary; 26 Scripps
Institute Oceanography/Photolibrary; 27t Ralph White/Corbis, b Dr Ken Macdonald/Science
Photo Library; 29 Lebrecht Music and Arts Picture Library/Corbis; 30-31 & 32 Shutterstock
Front cover: main image Mark Conlin/Photolibrary, below left to right: Marevision/Photolibrary,
Peter Batson/DeepSeaPhotography.com, Dante Fenolio/SPL

DAD0050
3-2011

9 8 7 6 5 4 3 2 1

Contents

Down in the Deep Sea

Light from the sun reaches only into the surface waters of the ocean. This upper layer of the sea is called the **sunlit zone**. It is about 655 feet (200 m) deep. Tiny floating plants live here. These are food for plant-eating sea creatures, which are eaten by larger fish.

This anglerfish, like many deep-sea fish, has a big gaping mouth and long teeth.

Amazing!

The average depth of the ocean is almost 2.5 miles (4 km).

Below the sunlit zone is the **twilight zone**, where there is a small amount of light. Then comes the darkest, deepest sea. There is no light at all in the water below 3,280 feet (1,000 m). Amazing creatures live here in total darkness. We know less about this area of the ocean than any other place on Earth.

Guess What?

The deepest part of the sea is a place called Challenger Deep in the Mariana Trench in the Pacific. It is about 36,000 feet (11,000 m) deep. Only one manned craft has ever been down there. This was the deep-diving vessel *Trieste* in 1960 with its two-man crew.

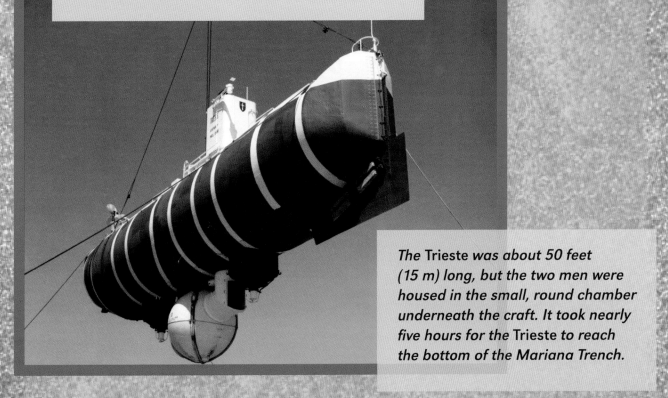

The Trieste *was about 50 feet (15 m) long, but the two men were housed in the small, round chamber underneath the craft. It took nearly five hours for the* Trieste *to reach the bottom of the Mariana Trench.*

The Twilight Zone

The twilight zone of the sea is between 655 feet (200 m) and 3,280 feet (1,000 m) down. There is some light, but it is not enough for plants to live on.

Some animals swim up to the sunlit waters to find food every day. Others eat each other or anything that drifts down from the surface. Many fish that live in the twilight zone have very large eyes to help them see even though there is very little light. The alfonsino fish and the hatchetfish are two such fish.

The comb jelly has rows of **luminous** hairs along its body. These beat to move through the water.

Some kinds of squid, jellyfish, and comb jellies are **transparent** (see-through), making it very hard for **predators** to see them.

Big Mouths

Not many creatures live in the deep sea, so food can be hard to find. Many deep-sea fish have extra-large mouths and can swallow almost anything they come across.

The grenadier, or rattail fish, lives in the deep sea. It has a big head and a thin body and tail. The gulper eel's mouth

The black swallower has a huge, stretchy stomach as well as a big mouth. This allows it to **digest** very large prey.

Amazing!

looks far too big for its long, thin body. It opens its huge jaws very wide and scoops up prey twice its size.

Another big-jawed hunter is the black sea devil, which has lots of long, sharp teeth. The sea devil is only 2.8 inches (7 cm) long, but it can swallow fish three times its size!

WATCH OUT!

Deep-sea trawling may harm many deep-sea fish. **Trawlers** drag large, heavy nets along the sea floor to catch everything in their path. Apart from fish, the nets catch many other creatures by accident.

The gulper eel's thin tail is so long that it sometimes gets tangled up!

Light in the Darkness

In the darkness of the deep sea, some creatures make their own light. They have special body parts that can produce light.

Lanternfish, dragonfish, and hatchetfish have lights along their bellies or sides. The lights make the outline of the fish's body hard to see and confuse predators. These fish may also use their lights to attract **mates**.

The viperfish uses light to help it catch prey. It has a very long ray on its back fin, which is tipped with a little flap. This flap makes light and shines in the darkness.

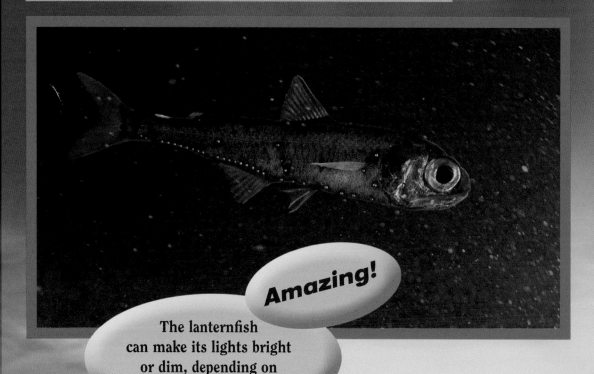

Amazing!

The lanternfish can make its lights bright or dim, depending on its surroundings.

When a deep-sea shrimp is attacked, it spits out a luminous liquid to confuse its attacker. Some liquid sticks to the predator, so its enemies can see it more easily.

Other fish are tempted to have a closer look at the flap in case it is something tasty to eat, but the sharp-toothed viperfish snaps them up.

The viperfish looks very fierce, but it is only about 12 inches (30 cm) long.

Seabed Animals

Some deep-sea creatures don't waste energy swimming around to find prey. They wait for prey to come to them. Sea lillies look like plants, but they are really animals. They stay in one place and catch bits of food that drift by with their long, feathery arms.

Sea cucumbers live on the floor of the deep sea. These animals are shaped like tubes. They are related to starfish and feed on scraps they find as they crawl around the seabed.

This deep-sea cucumber lives more than 6,560 feet (2,000 m) under the sea.

Amazing!

The Japanese giant spider crab lives on the seabed in deep water and is the biggest crab in the world. Its long legs span 13 feet (4 m)—that's more than two very tall humans lying head to toe.

A sea lily can grow new feathery arms if one arm is damaged.

The deep-sea lizardfish also likes to stay close to the sea floor, but it can quickly grab prey in its jaws.

Tripod fish can swim, but they spend much of their time standing on the sea floor on long, stiff fins. A tripod fish has special fins behind its head to help it sense anything drifting nearby that it might catch.

Guess What?

Did you know that sponges are animals? Glass sponges live on the floor of the deep sea and feed by **filtering** tiny creatures from the water. They are called glass sponges because the spiky skeleton is made of the same material as glass.

Dark Water

At depths greater than 3,280 feet (1,000 m), the sea is completely dark and very cold—close to freezing. The weight of the water above creates **pressure**, which most creatures cannot **survive**. Imagine trying to breathe with elephants sitting on top of you, and you will get the idea.

Deep-sea creatures are used to the high pressure, and most of them die if they are brought to the surface. One of the many strange creatures that lives in the deep sea is the dumbo octopus. Discovered in 2005, its name comes from its large fins that look like the ears of Dumbo, the elephant in the Disney film. The octopus moves by flapping these fins like wings.

The Dumbo octopus feeds on worms and shellfish that it swallows whole.

The deep-sea fangtooth fish has the biggest teeth for its body size of any animal. They're so big, it cannot close its mouth.

Amazing!

WATCH OUT!

Scientists have discovered that **pollution** from waste dumped in the sea is reaching the deepest depths. They have found **chemicals** in the bodies of deep-sea squid and other creatures.

Sperm Whales

Sperm whales dive deeper than any other whales. They often dive deeper than 6,560 feet (2,000 m) and stay there for over an hour, hunting prey such as squid. A sperm whale eats nearly 1 ton (1 t) of food every day.

Sperm whales can grow to 59 feet (18 m) long—that's longer than three family cars. Each whale has a huge head that is full of an oily liquid called spermaceti. This liquid becomes hard and waxy when it is cold.

The sperm whale has a square-shaped head up to 20 feet (6 m) long.

No one knows exactly why sperm whales have the liquid in their heads, but scientists think it may help them make deep dives and come back to the surface again.

WATCH OUT!

Fishermen used to hunt sperm whales for their spermaceti, which they used as oil and to make candles, soaps, and other products. Fewer sperm whales are now killed by hunters, but they can get caught in fishing lines and deep-sea cables. Ocean pollution also harms them.

A full-grown male sperm whale weighs 44 tons (40 t) or more—that's more than six elephants.

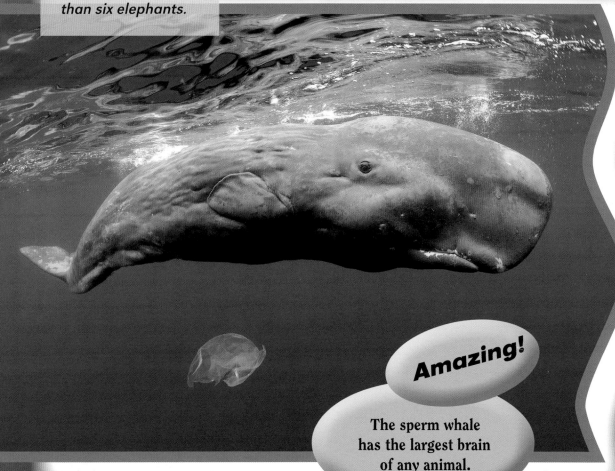

Amazing!

The sperm whale has the largest brain of any animal.

Deep-sea Giants

There have always been stories about giant sea monsters such as serpents and dragons. There may not be dragons in the deep sea, but there are some huge and extraordinary creatures.

One of the longest of all fish is the oarfish. Its body is shaped like a ribbon and can grow to 33 feet (10 m) long—almost as long as a bus. It has a long, red fin on its back.

Another deep-sea monster is the giant squid, which can grow to 40 feet (12 m) long. Giant squid have seldom been seen alive, but dead squid have been found in the stomachs of sperm whales.

The huge oarfish feeds on plankton and other small creatures that it strains from the water. It does not appear to have any teeth.

This jumbo squid is not quite as long as the giant squid, but it is a fierce hunter. The suckers on its tentacles are lined with sharp teeth, which help it grasp its prey.

Amazing!

A giant squid has the largest eyes of any animal. They are 12 inches (30 cm) across—bigger than a dinner plate.

Guess What?

Sperm whales and giant squid may have fierce battles when the whales are hunting the squid. Most sperm whales have scars made by the powerful **suckers** on the giant squid's long **tentacles**.

Bone-eating Worms

What do you think happens when a whale dies? Its body slowly sinks to the bottom of the sea. Many different kinds of creatures then feast on its huge body.

A female bone-eating worm is about the size of a human finger.

Amazing!

Male bone-eating worms are much smaller than females. The tiny males live inside the females.

Fish, crabs, and other animals feed on the dead whale's flesh until only the bones are left. Even these are food for some animals.

Worms called bone-eating snot-flower worms gather on the whale's skeleton. These worms bore into the bones to feed on the fat and oils inside.

The hagfish eats worms and other creatures that it finds by burrowing into the seabed.

Guess What?

Hagfish eat dead creatures such as whales. The hagfish does not have proper jaws. It bores into flesh with its toothed tongue and eats it away.

Finding a Mate

Finding a mate in the vast deep sea is not easy. Some fish do not let go when they do find a partner.

The male anglerfish is tiny compared to the female. He has patches on his head that help him track females by their smell. When he finds one, he attaches himself to her belly and stays there. He takes food from the female's blood. In return, he **fertilizes** her eggs.

Can you see the two little males attached to the back of this female anglerfish?

The hairy angler is a very strange-looking fish. Its body is covered with long spines and hairs that help it pick up the slightest movement in the water.

Amazing!

The football fish is a type of anglerfish with a body that is almost round. Male football fish, like other anglerfish, are much smaller than females.

WATCH OUT!
People used to think that waste dumped in the sea would sink to the bottom and stay there. Now we know that sea currents bring some of the waste to the surface again.

Deep-sea Sharks

The cookie-cutter shark is only about 20 inches (50 cm) long, but it attacks much larger animals.

Sharks are fierce ocean hunters, and some live in the deep sea. Many of these sharks spend the day in the dark depths. At night, they swim up nearer to the surface of the water where they feed.

The cookie-cutter shark gets its name from the way it attacks its prey. This shark latches on to a fish with its suckerlike jaws and digs in with its teeth. Then the shark spins its body around to

The huge megamouth shark is as long as a small car. This giant feeds mostly on tiny creatures and small fish that it filters from the water.

Amazing!

cut out a circle of flesh. Another deep-sea shark is the frill shark, which can grow to be 6.5 feet (2 m) long. Its large mouth is filled with as many as 300 three-pronged teeth—ideal for trapping prey.

WATCH OUT!
The goblin shark is one of the strangest looking sharks. It has a long snout with toothy jaws sticking out beneath. Its flabby body is pale pink!

Springs Under the Sea

In some places, huge springs of water gush out from the sea floor. This water is extremely hot and full of **minerals**. Most creatures cannot survive here, but scientists have discovered plenty of life around these deep-sea vents.

Bacteria live on the minerals in the water and other creatures feed on these bacteria. These include huge tube worms, which can grow to 6.5 feet (2 m) long.

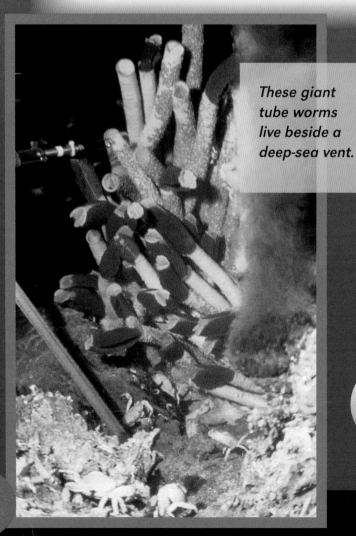

These giant tube worms live beside a deep-sea vent.

WATCH OUT!

Deep-sea vents do not last forever. Most gush for about 30 years before the water stops pouring out. Then the animals must move to another vent or die.

Amazing!

Giant vent mussels grow up to 12 inches (30 cm) long—that's three times the size of ordinary mussels.

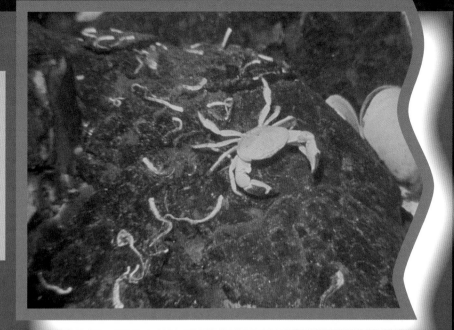

Vent crabs are some of the fiercest predators around deep-sea vents. They feed on bacteria and nibble on tube worms.

Pompeii worms also live near vents. They can stand hotter temperatures than any other animal. There are also special kinds of bacteria-eating mussels and clams as well as crabs that feed on other vent creatures.

A deep-sea fish swims among tube worms.

World Oceans: Pacific

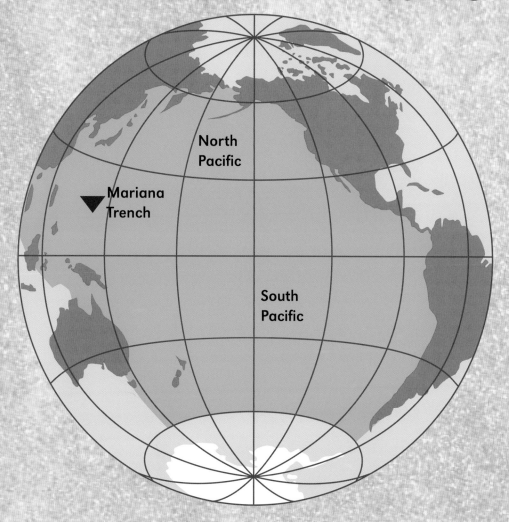

North
Pacific

Mariana
Trench

South
Pacific

The Pacific is the world's largest ocean. It covers about one-third of the surface of Earth and is nearly as big as all the land put together. The Pacific stretches from the Arctic in the north to the Southern Ocean in the south. It is bordered by the Americas and by Asia and Australia. The ocean includes seas such as the South China Sea and the Tasman Sea.

The Pacific Ocean covers an area about 15 times larger than the United States.

Pacific Facts

The deepest point in the Pacific is the Mariana Trench. About 36,000 feet (11,000 m) deep, it could hold Mount Everest, the world's highest mountain, with room to spare.

The average depth of the Pacific Ocean is just over 13,000 feet (4,000 m).

The Pacific is widest between Indonesia and the coasts of Colombia and Peru—a distance of about 12,300 miles (19,800 km).

There are at least 25,000 islands in the Pacific, which is more than in any other ocean.

Ocean explorer Ferdinand Magellan (c. 1480–1521) named the Pacific Ocean. He called the ocean *Tepre Pacificum*, which means peaceful sea.

The *Victoria* was one of five ships in Ferdinand Magellan's expedition to sail around the world. It was the only ship that completed the journey.

Glossary

bacteria
very tiny living things

chemicals
substances that are found in nature or made in a science laboratory; some chemicals are dangerous and can harm living things.

digest
to break down food so that it can be used by the body

fertilize
to bring eggs and male sperm together to make young

filter
to strain from water

luminous
something that makes its own light and shines in the dark

mate
Male and female animals pair up, or mate, to produce young; an animal's partner is its mate.

minerals
a substance such as calcium or zinc found in nature

pollution
things that dirty or damage the natural world, such as litter and oil

predator
an animal that hunts and kills other animals to eat

pressure
a force produced by pushing on something; in the deep sea, the weight of the water above produces pressure.

prey
an animal hunted and eaten by another animal

suckers
cup-shaped parts some animals use to cling to objects

sunlit zone
the top 655 feet (200 m) of the ocean that is lit by the sun

survive
to stay alive

tentacles
long, body parts that some animals use for feeling and grasping food

transparent
clear like glass and able to let light through

trawler
a kind of boat used for fishing

twilight zone
The twilight zone is between about 655 feet (200 m) and 3,280 feet (1,000 m) below the surface of the sea; there is a little light here, but the farther down, the darker it gets.

Index

FEB 1 5 2012